GREAT AMERICAN FIRE ENGINES

by J. MALLET

Translated from French by Marie-Claire Cournand

CRESCENT BOOKS
New York

INTRODUCTION

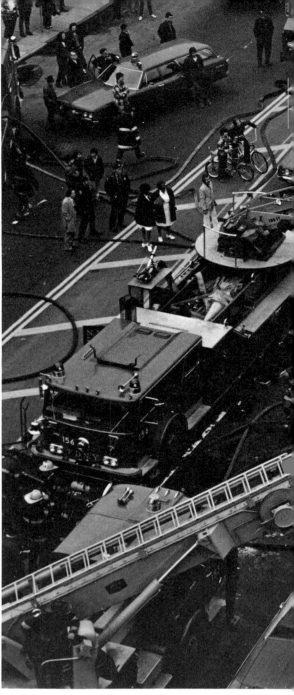

Power, extravagance, luxury, gaudiness, gadgetry, color; in the imagination of the average European, this is America. One word says it all: fascination. Of all the astonishing products of the new world, the American fire engine is perhaps one of the most picturesque. Because Europeans are accustomed to more sober fire-fighting vehicles, their fascination with the more colorful american variety is easy to understand. It seems, however, that Americans are no less interested in the subject, if we are to judge by the countless museums, associations, collections, publications and miscellaneous objects having to do with fire fighting that are to be found in the united states.

It is natural for the old world to wonder at the technological advances of the United States in the art of fire fighting. What is more surprising is the fact that Americans were by no means the pioneers in

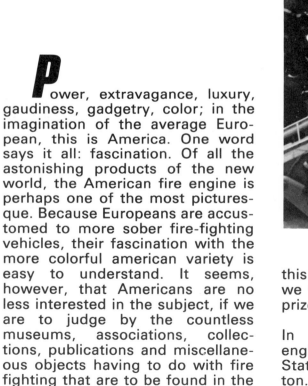

this field. If we look into the past, we find that England deserves the prize.

In 1679, the first known "fire engine" to be used in the United States made its appearance in Boston. This wooden hand-operated pump, imported from England, clearly won no popularity contests.

It was not until 1743 that Thomas Lote, an American, produced a fire engine that could compete with British-made Newshams (named after Richard Newsham), which

had been bought by New York and Philadelphia in 1731.

Volunteer brigades soon learned to appreciate the efficiency of this fire-fighting technique, and were anxious to buy apparatus of this type.

In 1829, a steam-operated pump was being used in England, but until the middle of the nineteenth century, American fire-fighters were still operating hand pumpers. Eleven years after George Braithwaite, with the help of John Erics-

son, had created the "Novelty" in London, Paul Rapsey Hodge, an American, built a steam pumper in New York City, but with only moderate success.

This resistance to progress in a nation known for its technological enterprise may seem surprising. It was due, in fact, to a strong reluctance on the part of volunteer fire companies to adopt the new steam-operated pumps. These men felt threatened by the new invention, and with good reason; for in order to use the new pump, it was

Mack's Aerialscope and a 100-ft. aerial ladder come to the rescue in Brooklyn, New York.

necessary to form professional fire brigades. Since the eighteenth century, volunteer firemen had held a great deal of influence in their communities, politically as well as economically and socially. Their influence was so great that it was impossible for public authorities to work against them. Not until a catastrophic fire devastated parts of southwest Ohio did the American public become aware of the inefficiency of fire-fighting techniques and realize the importance of changing the negative attitude of volunteer fire companies. As a result, a steam pumper was finally acclaimed on January 1, 1853, in Cincinnati.

This new fire engine was credited to Alexander B. Latta, a locomotive manufacturer, but it seems more likely now that his partner, Abel Shawk, was the real innovator. The Town Council of Cincinnati voted to subsidize this new vehicle for the sum of $ 5,000, and baptized it "Uncle Joe Ross" in honor of the Council member who had most done to obtain this grant. The suc-

cess of "Uncle Joe Ross" was so great that public donations for the sum of $ 13,400 were quickly raised for a second vehicle of this type.

This was to mark the beginning of a new era in fire figthing in the town of Cincinnati; with the advent of the steam pumper came the creation of the first professional fire company in the United States. Because the operation of this new machine required a far smaller work force, it was now possible for towns to finance their own fire departments.

In the 1650s, under the governorship of Peter Stuyvesant, New York City had already organized its own fire company; but it was not until the late eighteenth century, when Benjamin Franklin set up the first volunteer service in Philadelphia, that the towns and cities of the United States began to form volunteer departments in earnest, though without any clear administrative organization. The presence of several rival brigades within a city was a cause of healthy compe-

tition, although at times it also gave rise to unpleasant clashes, when the first volunteers to arrive on the scene tried to present their slower competitors from tackling the fire.

In the light of this attitude, and given the colossal fires that regularly devastated the new villages made of wood and canvas, many towns decided to follow the example of Cincinnati in setting up properly equipped, professional fire departments.

In America today, volunteer fire departments and call forces still outnumber professional companies; there are one thousand within a 93-mile radius of New York City.

Most of them have a long and colorful history, which may explain the remarkably gay appearance of their fire engines. Volunteer firemen are considered heroes in their towns, respected and admired; gifts and subsidies are showered upon their companies. As a result, they are often far better equipped

than professional departments in large cities, which are crippled by increasing financial problems, the victims more often than not being the firemen. The New York City Fire Department, with a force of 13,500, covering a population of 8,500,000, is the largest in the world, but has surprisingly outdated equipment.

At the beginning of this century, the transition to engine-driven fire vehicles was slow and arduous. Horse-drawn steam-operated pumps had become highly efficient in terms of maneuverability and power, some being capable of discharging 1,250 gallons per minutes (g.p.m.). Fire companies had bought a great deal of equipment and were anxious to get a return for their money. Fire chiefs, however, were quickly won over by the new technical advances and wanted engine-run vehicles for their departments.

Although we know for a fact that the first automotive fire engines were developed in France by Cap-

An International Fleetstar tanker equipped by Darley. This kind of apparatus holds 2,500 gal. of water.

tain Porteu de Rennes in 1898 and
in London by Merryweather & Son
in 1899, we cannot be as definite
as regards the United States. It is
popularly believed that this great
event took place in 1906, when the
Radnor Fire Company of Wayne,
Pennsylvania, put into service an
engine-driven vehicle produced by
the Waterous Engines Works of St.
Paul, Minnesota — a manufacturing concern still famous today for
its pumpers: from that time on,
interest in machines of this type
became general. But we do know
now that three years earlier, American LaFrance had delivered an
automotive hose-reel in New London, Connecticut, and that the fire
department of St. Louis was using
an electric fire engine.

Many manufacturers of that era
have since disappeared; others
regrouped to form what later
became American LaFrance. Some
developed and survived, and still
figure among the great names of
today, such as Seagrave, Pirsch,
Howe and Sutphen.

Nowadays, more than a hundred
companies are involved in the con-
struction of fire apparatus. Most of
these are small local companies,
whose market often never goes
beyond the borders of their county.
Their great number is due to the
sheer size of the United States and
to the availability of mass-produced pumps and general equipment, manufactured by specialists
such as Waterous and Hale. This
way, fire engines can be custom-
built to the needs and specifica-
tions of each individual client.

There also exist basic standard
models, of course. Equipment can
be mounted on mass-produced
commercial chassis specially adap-
ted for the purpose. But it is
very common nowadays for manufacturers to build custom-made
chassis from mass-produced components bought on the open market: engines, gearboxes, axles,
pumps and so on.

These vehicles always have extra-
powerful engines (usually diesels,

although the traditional gasoline
engine is still considered very efficient), which offer a number of
advantages. For example, they can
be mounted at the front, or better
still, in the middle of the pump,
allowing the pump and engine to
form a single unit. Easy access to
seating and the economical use of
volume and surface area are also
points in favor.

Unfortunately, there are disadvan-
tages also. Hoses, kept folded in
loops, are heavy and difficult to
handle: the crew is placed in an
open cab or on a platform at the
back, and exposed to all kinds of
bad weather and to the risks due to
road accidents and riots. For this
reason, some departments have
adopted closed cabs. Drivers often
have difficulty in holding the road
and have a limited view to the rear.

Because of the vast numbers of manufacturers, local preferences, special needs and frequently restricted budgets, American fire engines offer an infinite variety. We cannot do more than describe them in a general way, because the possibilities of technical combinations and fire-fighting methods are endless.

American fire-fighting apparatus mainly exports to Canada, Central and South America, and Saudi Arabia. The principal representatives of this industry are American LaFrance, Mack, Emergency One, FWD-Seagrave, Grumman-Howe-Oren, Pierce, Pirsch, Darley, Boardman, Sutphen, Crown, F.M.C.-Van Pelt, Ward LaFrance, Maxim, Hahn and Young. Mass-produced standard chassis are produced by International, Chevrolet, Ford, GMC and Mack, and custom-made chassis by American LaFrance, Duplex-Drive, Mack, Crown, Pirsch, Pierce, Hendrickson, FWD, Oshkosh and Pemfab.

Aerial ladders are either American-made by such companies as Seagrave, Pirsch, American LaFrance, Maxim, Emergency One and, more recently, Mack and Ladder Towers; or imported from the firms Magirus, Metz, Morita and Geesink. Most elevating platforms and aerial towers are manufactured by Snorkel and Calavar.

This Duplex fire engine is equipped by Darley. Note the top-mounted control panel behind the cab, which allows firemen to operate without getting off the truck. This system, as well as the double closed cab used by the Duplex, are growing increasingly popular.

The similarity in names, American LaFrance and Ward LaFrance, might seem to suggest that these two manufacturers are in some way associated. This is not the case. While it is true that the founders of these companies were members of the same family and that both are based in Elmira, New York, there has never been any collaboration or other connection between them. In fact, these two companies are powerful rivals.

American LaFrance, founded in 1832, has been in existence for over one hundred and fifty years. This is a most remarkable fact. Aside from the Merryweather and Bachert companies, founded respectively in England in 1692 and in Germany in 1830, no other fire equipment manufacturer has existed for quite so long. Such is the reputation of American LaFrance that the name of this company has become to fire engines what General Motors is to the automobile.

American LaFrance has been known under this name since 1903. From 1832 until that date, the company had gone through a series of mergers and take-overs which account for the many changes in its commercial status. If we examine the geneological tree of American LaFrance, we recognize many names which were relatively famous at the time of the first hand and steam-operated pumpers. Rogers, Button, Latta Lane and Bodley had joined in partnership in 1768, te become the Ahrens Manufacturing Company; in 1891, they merged with Silsby, Clapp and Jones and formed the American Fire Engine Company. The LaFrance Fire Engine Company refused at the time to become part of this group. Truckson LaFrance, a descendant of French Huguenots from Pennsylvania, had settled in Elmira in 1860. He came from a family of industrialists whose real name — Hyenveux — was considered unpronounceable in English; for this reason they changed it to LaFrance.

Truckson LaFrance developed a passionate interest for steam pumps and, in 1873, founded a company which eventually became the LaFrance Fire Engine Company.

In 1900, five years after Truckson's death, the International Fire Engine Company was formed, joining all the manufacturers of fire equipment in the country, including the American and LaFrance Fire Engine Companies. Three years later, in an attempt to clear up its finances, the International Fire Engine Company, named after its two most important associates, was born.

Cris Ahrens left the company almost immediately and was soon followed by Charles Fox, chief mechanic for American LaFrance. In 1908, they formed the Ahrens-Fox Fire Engine Company, which to this day remains famous for its legendary pumpers, long considered the "Rolls-Royces" of fire engines; their quality was such that some of them are still in use today. This, unfortunately, did not prevent Ahrens-Fox from meeting

FREEPORT SNORKEL NO. 1

with financial problems, and, in 1956, the company was taken over by Mack.

The success of American LaFrance is partly due to its long history of fire fighting, but more especially to its technical innovations in this field of American industry. From the beginning, it has always been a pioneer, presenting American firemen with their first ladder in 1882, and later their first light truck. In 1929, it introduced vehicles with four-wheel brakes and left-hand drive and, in 1935, the first American all-steel hydraulic ladder. Three years later, American LaFrance sold Los Angeles two Metropolitan Duplex super-pumpers, equipped with two 250 h.p. V12 engines and two 1500 g.p.m. pumps. These fires engines, considered gigantic at the time, remained in service until 1963.

American LaFrance produces fire engines of every possible size and description; it manufactures all its components and for this reason can satisfy all the needs of its customers. A journalist once wrote that the wouldn't be surprised if ALF should start providing its cus-

tomers with dalmatians, which traditionally serve as mascots for American firemen. The management, not lacking in humor, answered that it would be delighted to honor such a request.

In order to reduce costs, it is possible to mount ALF equipment on mass-produced rather than special chassis. In 1964, the Pioneer was put on the market to fill the gap between more sophisticated custom-made vehicles and the standard commercial apparatus.

American fire engines have a character and appearance all their own, and manufacturing methods and practices are different from those of any other country. Standards have been laid down by the National Fire Protection Association, but these apply mainly to the efficiency of hydraulic systems; much less is said concerning chassis and other equipment. Furthermore, these are recommendations rather than regulations. Pump discharge capacity is the only standard feature by which vehicles can be put into categories. Parallel series of centrifugal pumps are classified according to the number of

15

A Ward LaFrance for the connoisseur!

Since 1974, the largest Ward LaFrance pumpers (1,750 g.p.m.) can be equipped with a diesel engine.

An elegantly fitted-out Century, by Ward LaFrance.

This rear view of an American LaFrance gives us an idea of the lengths of ladder and hose equipment that can be carried by a fire truck.

Ladder trucks are particular to the United States. This American LaFrance is equipped with a rear seat for the tillerman.

gallons which they discharge per minute, at an average pressure of 150 p.s.i. (pounds per square inch). According to this, standard fire pump sizes for installation on apparatus are 500 g.p.m., 750 g.p.m., 1,000 g.p.m., 1,250 g.p.m., 1,500 g.p.m., 1,750 g.p.m., 2,000 g.p.m. Note that these rates of discharge are much highter than in any other country; the pumps seem to have been designed for large towns with an inexhaustible water supply, without much thought for rural and semi-rural areas.

The last few years have seen the appearance of more and more powerful and highly automated vehicle. These have been developed in response to the need to cut back on personnel, due to the enormous cost of maintaining a professional fire department.

Pumps produced by American LaFrance are different from those of any other manufacturer, who generally buy equipment from Hale, Waterous, Darley and F.M.C.-John Bean (specialists in high-pressure pumps). One exclusive ALF feature used by may fire departments is the Twinflow, a two-level centrifugal pump with a discharge rate of 500 to 2,000 g.p.m.

The different models manufactured by ALF are usually classified by serial numbers (800, 900, 1,000). One model, put on the market in 1973, was baptized the Century in honor of two centennial celebrations: the one hundredth anniversary of the first congress of Baltimore fire chiefs, and the creation of the LaFrance Engine Co. at Elmira.

The Century was the first mass-produced custom-built fire engine; until then, all fire chassis had been made to order. Because of its bold design, it is still popular today. The cab is placed in front of the engine, rather than behind it, as in most commercial vehicles, and can carry up to five men far more safely than in any other type of cab. This fire engine is very easy to handle thanks to its reduced turning-circle, and is equipped with a Detroit Diesel, a pump with a discharge of 1,000 to 2,000 g.p.m., according to specification, and a 500 gal. water tank. The Century can be mounted with various ALF equipment: extinguishing foam guns,

The success of this airport crash truck (1,000 g.p.m.) helped American LaFrance to regain its place on the market.

aerial ladders, elevating platforms or wate towers.

Although American LaFrance continues to manufacture tractor-drawn aerial ladders, the most characteristic feature of American fire-fighting equipment, their use is on the decline. Today, more and more departments are adopting the less cumbersome modular European models.

This company also manufactures airport crash trucks.

Since 1966, American LaFrance has been a member of the ATO, an organization which engages in a great range of activities; the same is true of the Snorkel Fire Equipment Company, which specialized in elevating platforms.

In memory of the French origins of its founder. Ward LaFrance has adopted the fleur-de-lis as its trademark.

In 1918, A. Ward LaFrance opened a manufacturing factory for commercial rather than fire-fighting vehicles. Later, he became interested in heavy equipment and made his contribution to the war effort by offering the army a great number of M1 and M1A1 wreckers as well as 6 × 4 and 6 × 6 military trucks.

In 1931, Ward LaFrance produced its first fire engine, and this soon became the company's main activity. Until 1960, however, it continued to manufacture commercial vehicles also.

In 1954, the Fireball was put on the market and was well received by fire departments with limited budgets. This new model offered two advantages: it was less expensive than other fire engines and could be delivered relatively quickly. The Fireball, mounted on a specially conceived WLF chassis, carried a standard 500 g.p.m. pump and a 500 gal. water tank, and could include various other equipment.

In 1960, WLF added the Firebrand to its list. This vehicle, which came with a closed or open forward cab (the "cabover"), was not as successful as its predecessor.

In 1959, when Ward LaFrance decided to adopt the cabover, many of its chassis included Cin-

A 50-ft. Tele-Squrt mounted on a Pioneer by American LaFrance.

An American LaFrance "quint" equipped with a 100-ft. ladder.

Preceding pages: A windscreen at the back of this open-cab American LaFrance pumper protects standing firemen from the wind. The hard suction hoses behind the control panel are used to draw water from lakes and rivers.

cinnati cabs, so-named because they were built in this Ohio city by the Truck Cab Equipment Company. Because these types of cabs have become popular with many manufacturers, it is often difficult to distinguish between vehicles of different brands.

Aside from mounting standard and custom equipment on its own chassis, Ward LaFrance supplies such companies as Ford, International and Chevrolet.

For the last twenty years or so, the Ward LaFrance Truck Corporation has specialized in airport crash trucks and has sold a great many fire engines of this type.

In 1972, WLF teamed up with the US Steel Corporation, one of the largest metallurgical concerns in the world, and designed a new fire engine whose ultra-modern style caused a sensation. The original Vantage, mounted on a Ford C-900 chassis and powered by a Ford V8 engine, had a 1000 g.p.m. pump and a water tank capacity of 750 gal. The Vantage could carry seven firemen in a European-style closed cab which tipped over for easier access to the engine. This vehicle was painted lime-green yellow. Although the first fire engives

in America were painted red-brown or sometimes white, red had been adopted as the standard color by the time of the First World War. It was inevitable, of course, in this vast country where local influences are so strong, that other colors should be used; still, this happened quite rarely.

In 1972, Ward LaFrance, in an effort to compete with its powerful rival company American LaFrance, situated a mere stone's throw across a river branch, contacted the advertising agents Shaw Elliott in New York, and asked them for an idea.

Since both companies' products were of equally good quality, the only possible solution was to adopt an aggressive publicity campaign. The agency tried to come up with some technical advantage that would give their client and edge over the rival company. It was then that they brought forward the research carried out several years previously by the ophthalmologist Dr. Stephen, S. Solomon, into the color effectiveness of fire engines.

This scientist, a volunteer fireman, had demonstrated that red was barely visible at night or in bad weather, and had further esta-

blished that lime-green yellow was the most effective color.

Ward LaFrance then distributed a lenghty questionnaire to every corner of the United States, partly in order to establish the circumstances surrounding accidents caused by poor visibility, and partly to test the opinions of fire chiefs regarding the unusual new color — although airport crash trucks had been painted yellow as early as 1949.

The idea met with such rapid approval that, some time later, a Missouri officer was prompted to declare, "Red is dead." Forty percent of WLF's new fire engines were painted yellow, although many of the larger professional departments rejected the idea, preferring to keep to the traditional color. In 1975, more than on hundred and forty-five fire departments in the United States ordered lime-green yellow fire apparatus. Salvador, Columbia, Venezuela and Saudi-Arabia soon followed suit. Since that time, the trend away from red fire engines has grown steadily, going beyond simple safety considerations and into the realm of pure effect. Some fire engines are even painted in the colors of the American flag by their patriotic crews.

New York City, Cincinnati, Los Angeles, San Francisco and Philadelphia have remained faithful to the traditional red, but they are exceptions rather than the rule. Most fire departments have adopted yellow or white, or varying shades of orange, as the basic color for their fire trucks — not to mention even more unexpected colors such as blue, silvergray, green, black, purple or bronze.

In cities where fire companies are administered by different authorities, it is customary for them to use fire apparatus of varying colors, so they can be more easily recognized.

In 1979, Ward LaFrance took over the Maxim Motors Company, which had been administered by FWD-Seagrave since 1956.

As early as 1914, Maxim was building fire engines from a factory in Middleboro, Massachusetts. In 1952, the company obtained a license for the use of German-made Magirus ladders, and mounted them on its own chassis. Maxim has always specialized in ladders, and was already selling its first models in 1888. Until the recent take-over, many were sold to Mack and to Ward LaFrance.

Maxim has always been famous for its quality ladders.

MACK

Rear view of an Aerialscope.

BULLDOG 1

Mack's new 107-ft. aerial ladder is mounted on a Bulldog I.

Mack is the main supplier of the New York City Fire Department.

The new Mack MC pumper, equipped with a diesel made by the Swedish company Scania-Vabis.

The original Mack B was driven by a 200 h.p. gasoline engine. After 1960, most were equipped with Thermodyne diesels.

Since 1979, Mack has been handling medium-duty trucks made by Renault vehicles industriels, and distributing them all over the United States.

The original Mack company was founded by five brothers of German heritage, whose family had been established in the United States for three generations. Of the five, Jack Mack was the most adventurous and imaginative. In 1900, in the borough of Brooklyn, he built a vehicle entirely by hand, and for this reason has always been considered the company's real founder.

The first commercial Mack vehicle was a twenty-passenger bus with chain drive and a four-cylinder Mack engine. It ran efficiently for seventeen years and was retired after covering a total of one million miles!

The success of this first venture forced the Mack brothers to seek better facilities and, in 1905, they moved their operations to Allentown, Pennsylvania.

The Mack Brothers Motor Car Company grew by leaps and bounds and, in 1911, merged with the Saurer Motor Car Co., forming the International Motor Car Company. Soon afterwards, they were joined by the Hewitt Motor Co.

During World War I, Mack's reputation was further established by the thousands of A.C. trucks that it delivered to the American Army. The short, squat hoods and sturdy qualities of these trucks soon earned them the nickname of "Bulldogs" from the English. This name has stuck, and remains Mack's trademark today. The A.C. was manufactured for twenty years; its reputation throughout the world can only be compared to that of the Model T Ford.

The A.C. was frequently used as a fire engine. A great number of army-surplus Bulldogs were fitted with fire-fighting equipment, and

Mack is unquestionably the most famous name in American trucks in the world. It is known for its great variety of vehicles, which range from commercial and military trucks to public works apparatus and fire engines. It has branches in Canada, Pakistan, Iran, Australia and Venezuela, and once ran in France. The traditional quality of Mack trucks has made their bulldog emblem famous all over the world.

remained in service until the 1960s.

Since 1922, when the company changed its name to Mack Trucks Inc., each truck has carried the emblem of the bulldog: golden bulldogs are used for Mack-made engines, chrome for those made by other manufacturers (Scania, Cummins, Detroit Diesel, Caterpillar).

The year Mack merged with Saurer, it received its first orders for fire engines. At the end of 1911, the first pumper chassis was built for the town of Bala-Cynwyd, near Philadelphia. From then on, Mack was a name among fire engine manufacturers, quickly developing in this branch of its activities and producing fire pumpers mounted on its won brand of equipment.

The perfecting of various techniques has given Mack an important role in the development of fire-fighting apparatus. One of its most significant contributions was a 2000 g.p.m. pumper which made

its appearance in Minneapolis in 1935 and was considered gigantic for its time. The same year, Mack created the "sedan cab" which was closed, therefore ensuring greater safety to its occupants. The thermodyne diesel engine, conceived in 1959 for the Mack B, was greatly successful and marked the beginning of a new era in fire vehicles.

From the heritage of Ahrens Fox, which was taken over in 1956, was born the Mack C, equipped with a cabover, pumps discharging from 500 to 1,250 g.p.m. and 65-to 100-ft, aerial ladders.

In the 1960s, the Allentown-based company produced two revolutionary new fire trucks. With its telescopic boom, the Aerialscope combined the advantages of the aerial ladder and the efficiency of the elevating platform, which can carry more equipment. It was equipped with two high-pressure monitor nozzles for elevated fire stream service, whereas aerial ladders have

This Mack truck, mounted with a 100-ft. American LaFrance aerial ladder, serves the island of Manhattan.

27

This rescue squad truck, custom-built by Ranger Truck Bodies, is equipped with a 1,500 g.p.m. pump, 40 gal. of emulsifiers and a 450 gal. water tank. It also carries rescue equipment.

A typical example of the American fire engine: a Mac CF, with 1,250 g.p.m. pump and a 500 gal. water tank.

The "torpedo" cab, seen here on a Mack R, is relatively rare. Note the fireman's helmet worn by the bulldog on the side of fire engine.

This 1,000 g.p.m. pumper carries the Aerialscope, a relatively rare combination.

The Mack Super Pumper and Super Tender, made for the city of New York. Note the powerful deck gun pointed over the tender cab.

only only one. At its full height, the Aerialscope could reach 75 ft.

The first fire truck of this kind was bought in 1964 by the New York City Fire Department, a long-time customer equipped almost exclusively by Mack. In 1974, the company celebrated the delivery to New York City of its one thousandth Aerialscope.

Mack's most spectacular achievement, however, remains the gigantic Mack Super Pumper System, which made its apperance in New York City in 1965. It is unquestionably the most powerful pumper in the world and was designed with the help of Gibbs & Fox, a shipbuilding company.

The Super Pumper is driven by a British-made 2,400 h.p. Napier Deltic diesel engine, which weighs nearly six tons. Its De Laval pump

has an unbelievable nominal rating of 8,800 g.p.m. and discharges through 6-in. hoses laid by the Super Tender — an auxiliary vehicle which also carries the couplings, adapters and other accessories that make the giant operational. The Super Tender is equipped with a monitor nozzle so powerful (9,775 g.p.m.) that the truck has to be fitted with hydraulic jacks for stabilization purposes. The outfit is completed by three Mack satellite tenders, each equipped with deck guns that can discharge 4,000 g.p.m. Like the Super Tender, they can each lay 2,000 ft. of 6-in. hoses.

Mack specializes in heavyweight road trucks, but also offers a large variety of heavy-duty fire pumpers.

All kinds of fire apparatus is made by this company except pumps and ladders. Pumps are provided by Hale and ladders by Conestoga Customs Products, but all are manufactured according to specification. On demand, any engine can be installed in a Mack truck.

Among its new apparatus, Mack now offers for the first time a 107-ft, ladder which is mounted,

European-style, on a CF chassis, named the Bulldog I in an attempt to gain widespread popularity. Mack also offers a lighter and more economical pumper, the Mid-Liner. With a pump that discharges 750 to 1,000 g.p.m. according to specification, and a 500 gal. water-tank, the Mid-Liner can be classified as an attack pumper.

It is interesting to note that the Mid-Liner's MS 200 chassis is manufactured at Renault Véhicules Industriels in Blainville, France. The two companies have made agreements under which Mack distributes the Renault medium-duty commercial range in the United States under its own name.

The MS 200 had previously been adopted by the Fire Power and Equipment Co. in Orlando, Florida. This company is a subsidiary of Central Florida Mack Trucks, Inc. and, as a result, ninety-eight percent of its chassis are by Mack. It also distributes fire vehicles that are entirely fitted out by the Allentown company.

The MS 200 equipped by the Fire Power and Equipment Co. is called the Equalizer.

EMERGENCY ONE

the United States is a remarkable success story.

In less than then years, it has cornered twenty percent of the market and ranks among the three giants in the industry: American LaFrance, Mack and Seagrave.

The amazing growth of this company is all the more surprising when we consider that its founder, Bob Wormser, had no previous knowledge whatsoever of fire fighting. He started his company in 1974 without the benefit of his competitors' long years of experience in the field, in Ocala, Florida, thousands of miles away from the traditional strongholds of the fire-fighting industry. These factors, considered at the time to be hopeless obstacles, have in fact contributed to Emergency One's huge success.

Bob Wormser, a manufacturer of sports equipment, retired to Florida in 1970 and, after some thought, decided to break into an entirely new field. At first, he considered the possibilities of rescue vehicles. His idea was to manufacture a modular body that could easily be mounted on an ordinary pickup truck, converting it into an instant rescue vehicle for transporting the wounded. Federal law, however, prevented him from carrying out his plans and he was forced to turn his attentions elsewhere.

This was the time of the great fuel crisis. Oil prices and labor costs were rising rapidly and gasoline shortages were creating a panic in the auto industry. It soom became apparent to Wormser that tackling this problem was his best chance of success. Vehicles with low fuel consumption and lower-priced fire apparatus were urgently needed. Convinced that fire departments across the country were bound to realize this sooner or later, Wormser decided to move in this direction.

For the founder of Emergency One, this could well be the key to success. In spite of his confidence and

*T*he spectacular rise of this manufacturing company proves beyond doubt that a traditional brand name and long years of experience in fire fighting are not the only keys to success in the fire equipment industry. In this area as in so many others, the same result can be achieved by a high spirit of enterprise, a steady flow of new ideas and the effective use of the latest technology.

The recent establishment of Emergency One as an important manufacturer of heavy-duty material in

Opposite page: The Stratospear by Emergency One is basically a British-made Simon elevating platform.

the positive contacts with municipal and public works acquired previously, he also knew that one great stumbling block lay in his was: he was a newcomer. In order to succedd, he must spare no efforts to make his company known to the fire-fighting community. This closed world was difficult to conquer; and the only way to win the battle was to offer something new and revolutionary.

He guaranteed a waiting period of not more than two months for his prefabricated models and six months for custom-built apparatus; no other manufacturer could deliver in so short a time.

In order to keep to his promise, Wormser had to maintain a permanent supply of all different kinds of apparatus, including chassis; Crown Firecoach, for instance, can wait up to nine months for delivery of an Allison automatic transmission.

Emergency One took the risk of stocking all the necessary equipment for its fire trucks and immediately bought fifty GMC chassis. This commercial maneuver went against the policies of all Wormser's competitors who considered such a system far too expensive.

The investment proved highly successful. The Ocala-based company now keeps a permanent supply of one hundred and fifty chassis made by GMC, Ford, Hendrickson, Pemfab and Duplex, and more Hale pumps than its own manufacturer.

In an attempt to make up for his relative lack of experience in the filed, Bob Wormser launched a spectacular publicity campaign through advertising media aimed not only at firemen but available to the general public.

Today, Emergency One, now a subsidiary of the Federal Signal Corporation, is still growing rapidly and generating an endless stream of new ideas.

Recently the company brought out three new features in its Stratospear series; these include a 55-ft., telescopic boom and a 100-ft. British-made Simon elevating platform with an 880 lb. payload, topped by a 100-ft. aluminium ladder, the highest ever built in the United States. The entire unit is mounted on a Hendrickson chassis.

Emergency One apparatus is almost exclusively made of aluminium. This element, more expensive than stainless steel but far ligther, can be mounted on smaller and less expensive chassis; because of its lighter weight, fire trucks can carry more equipment and more water.

The technicians at Emergency One are convinced of the practical advantages and reliability of aluminium; firemen, however, remain somewhat skeptical as to its resistance to wear, severe weather conditions and difficult maneuvers.

Every type of vehicle is made by this company: light or heavyweight rescue or "squad" trucks, tankers with a capacity of 1,250 to 3,000 gal. "mini" and "quick attack" pumpers — small emergency vehicles, usually mounted on pickup trucks and equipped with a 250 g.p.m. pump and 250 to 300 gal. water tank. The "midipumper" is slightly more powerful.

All pump-equipped vehicles that can discharge 500 to 2,000 g.p.m., depending on the model, qualify as pumpers.

The most widely used type of apparatus in America is the "tripe combination" pumper, a three-functional vehicle equipped with pump, hoses and water tank. The length and size of the hoses vary from one fire department to another, ranging from 250 ft. (1·5-in. diameter) to 1,830 ft. (2·5-in.). Roughly half of these vehicles have a tank capacity of 250 to 400 gal. They also carry a 16-ft. folding hook ladder, a 25-ft. ground ladder and rescue equipment. It is now more and more common to find models equipped with high-pressure monitor nozzles for use in major fires.

A considerable number of triple combination pumpers carry telescopic or articulated booms, known as "Squrts".

The "quad" (a four-functional vehicle) and the "quint" (a five-functional vehicle) are both powerful, and offer a wide range of possibilities; for these reasons they are very popular in small communities. Unfortunately, if one piece of equipment breaks down, the whole vehicle can be out of action.

The "quad" is basically a triple-combination pumper, but carries 200 ft. of ground ladders in addition to its usual equipment. If a power-operated aerial ladder or elevating platform is added, such apparatus is termed a "quint". In spite of the versatility of this fire engine, there tends to be a decrease in operating efficiency and capability if too many functions are performed by one unit of apparatus.

There are two types of forest fire trucks. One, basically a "triple", has four-wheel drive and carries a high-pressure booster pump with a rating of 580 p.s.i. This pump allows water to be discharged while the vehicle is in motion. The other type is simply a van with two removable units, a water tank and a pump, which can be slid into place when required. A certain proportion of these are reconditioned army vehicles.

The largest fleets of forest fire-fighting vehicles are operated by the US Forest Service, the Department of Agriculture and Bureau of Land Management. Besides the above-mentioned apparatus, these services also use Jeeps with fire pumps mounted on the front and double-shared trenching plows for cutting fire lines. A 92-gal. tank is mounted on a trailer.

Ultimately, this combination of vehicles and equipment used to combat forest fires is insufficient: no ground truck is capable of fighting a major fire in America's vast expanses of forest. This is why the forest services prefer to use bulldozers to isolate the fire, and then extinguish it by means of aircraft carrying water or fire-retardant agents. Meanwhile, teams of foresters using fairly light equipment attack the fire from the ground.

These men sometimes spend long and exhausting hours traveling to the fire; for this reason helicopters are being used more and more to transport them to the scene.

Some foresters have been trained to use parachutes. Their number, however, is declining as the call for helicopters increases.

Special apparatus can have any number of purposes. Their chassis, body-work and equipment vary widely, and it seems that each fire department has its own models and its own methods, depending on particular needs.

The average American fire department is usually equipped with two triple-combination pumpers, an aerial ladder or elevating platform, a "squad" and a staff command vehicle carrying radio communications facilities. The American system prefers a number of small fire substations within a given area to larger centers, spaced further apart and more heavily equipped.

Although more than a hundred manufacturers of fire equipment exist in America today, many fire departments build their own vehicles. This brush truck carries the Smokey the Bear emblem.

A gasoline tank is being cooled by an Emergency One mini-pumper.

A lime-green yellow midi-pumper by Emergency One; this new color has high visibility characteristics.

The top-of-the-line in Emergency One pumpers: the Protectors IV.

The latest aerial ladder by Emergency One is 110 ft high.

THE VETERANS

In the days of horse-drawn pumps, there were many fire equipment manufacturers in the United States. With the advent of the automobile at the turn of the century, many of these went bankrupt. Those companies which managed to survive — Seagrave, Sutphen and Howe-Oren-Grumman — have nearly all existed for over a century and, through the years, have left their mark on a wide range of fire-fighting apparatus.

The Peter Pirsch & Sons Company, one of the oldest in the field, has an excellent reputation among American firement for turning out quality products.

In 1857 Peter Pirsch opened his factory in Kenosha, Wisconsin, where the better-known giant American Motors Corporation is also located.

Pirsch, an experienced volunteer fireman, soon became aware of the deficiencies and dangers of ladder equipment used by fire departments, and decided to build his own. He then examined a new ladder which had been created three years before the great Chicago fire of 1871 by the head mechanic of the San Francisco Fire Department, Daniel B. Hayes. In those days, new ideas conceived elsewhere than in New York had little chance of success. In 1882, Hayes sold his patent to American La France.

Hayes' system was roughly the following : a metal rod at the bottom of the ladder's frame was controlled by a nut and bolt assembly; when the nut was turned by hand, the rod allowed the ladder to extend to its full height.

At the time, this innovation gave Pirsch much food for thought. From then on he was committed to the development and improvement of the fire ladder. In 1931, he created the first all-aluminium hydraulic ladder. Four years later, Kenosha sold a 100-footer to the town of Melrose, Massachusetts, where it was used until 1971.

In 1928, seven years before any of his competitors, Pirsch had put into service the first closed-cab pumper in the United States.

Since 1922, Pirsch's manufacturing company has offered a complete range of fire apparatus mounted on chassis of different brands; in 1926, he began to produce his own chassis. Ladder equipment, however, continues to be the specialty of the Peter Pirsch & Sons Company.

In the United States, ladder height ranges from 60 to 100 ft. They are mounted either on the truck itself or on a trailer drawn by a tractor vehicle. Traditionally, turntables are positioned in the middle of the chassis, with the ladder pointing towards the back of the vehicle. But the European method of

This 90-ft Seagrave platform is articulated in two places; Most elevating platforms in America have only one break.

mounting the turntable at the rear, with the ladder resting on top of the cab, is becoming increasingly popular. Ladder trucks, the most characteristic feature of American fire vehicles, have always been great favorites with fire departments of this country because of their high maneuverability in cities and the fact that they are able to carry large amounts of other necessary apparatus, including ventilation units and, in some cities, rescue and salvage equipment. A seat is mounted at the rear for the tillerman, whose job is to operate the trailer's contra-steering wheels, which is extremely difficult.

Nevertheless, trailer-drawn ladders are on the decline. Fire departments have discovered that the European method allows them to carry just as much but in a less cumbersome way; and, most important of all, it makes the vehicle much more stable.

Elevating platforms and aerial towers are very widely used in this country. The first person to propose that they serve as fire-fighting equipment was Captain Quinn of Chicago. Their height usually varies from 50 to 100 ft, but on some models, such as Calavar's Firebird, they can rise to 150 ft. The marine fire department of the port of Marseille has recently bought this latest model and is proud to own the highest elevating platform not only in France, but in all of Europe.

Originally, this apparatus was built to serve in rescue operations, but it was discovered that aerial ladders appeared more reassuring to the victim. As a result, the platform is rarely used nowadays for this purpose. The platform, however, offers an efficient means of extinguishing fires; the bucket can carry several men as well as equipment, and elevated fire stream service is provided through metal pipes. Snorkel is the leading manufacturer of this type of apparatus, and its name has grown famous all over the world.

The success of the elevating platform inspired Snorkel to create the Squrt, which has grown extremely popular in recent years. It consists in a telescopic or articulated boom, rarely exceeding 50 ft, in height, which feeds a very powerful moni-

In spite of its old-fashioned appearance, this Pirsch, currently used in Pennsylvania, was built as recently as 1968. It is painted red-brown, which was the original color of American fire engines.

The main competitor of Mack's Aerialscope: the Aerial Tower by Sutphen.

This Grumman Customcat is less than six feet high, which allows it easy access to the new San Francisco Airport's underground areas. Low-silhouette fire engines are also used in underground parking lots.

This attack pumper, mounted on a GMC 4 × 4, is called a Firecat, following Grumman's traditional practice of giving feline names to its US fighter planes.

A certain number of pumpers were latter equipped with 40 to 50-ft. elevating platforms.

The 750 g.p.m. discharge capacity of this Seagrave pump is considered relatively low in the United States. In countries such as France, the most powerful pumpers are rated at 2,000 liters per minute (528.4 g.p.m.).

tor nozzle and is controlled from the ground at an angle. As a consequence, firemen can direct massive quantities of water at a fire from a safe distance; and when we consider that many American warehouses are brick and metal structures, this is a great advantage. Furthermore, the boom is so mobile that it can be directed downwards onto the fire, or upwards, through the openings, into the building.

The telescopic model has the added feature of an access ladder; it is called the "Tele-Squrt" and can reach 75 ft. The Squrt and the Tele-Squrt are varieties of the water tower, a great favorite with American firemen.

The Mobile Aerial Company, based in Fort Wayne, Indiana, manufactures another type of boom-operated fire apparatus, the High-Ranger. Two of these are used on the famous Marseille fireboat, the Louis Colet.

The Seagrave Corporation, along with Mack and American LaFrance, is one of the three best-known fire engine builders in the United States. It is also one of the oldest companies and has recently celebrated its 100th anniversary.

In 1881, Frederic Seagrave of Detroit, Michigan, began to manufacture ladders — not for fire-fighting purposes but for use in orchards. Volunteer firemen in the city often borrowed them to supplement their equipment; seeing this, Seagrave decided to manufacture specially built ladders for fire purposes. Ten years later, he moved his factory to Columbus, Ohio.

Like Peter Pirsch, Seagrave was familiar with the Hayes ladder, and, like him, he based his research into possible improvements on this basic model. His aim was to reduce the number of men needed to raise ladders to their full height, and he invented a system of crank-operated springs, which turned out to be a far easier and quicker method.

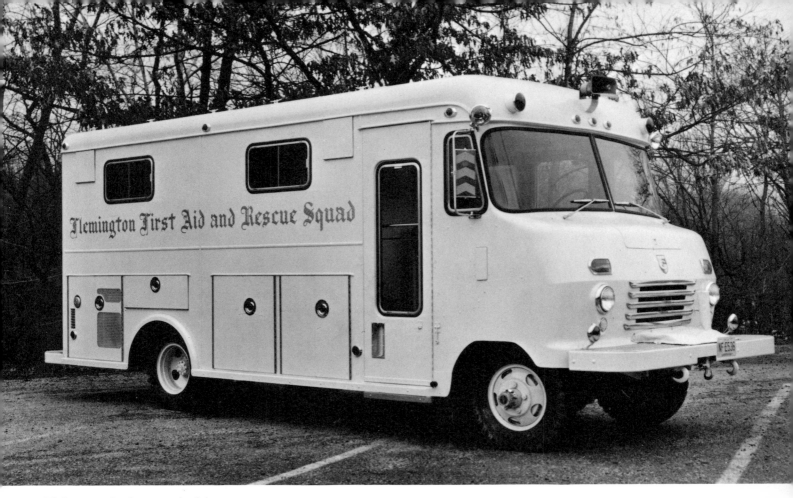

This revolutionary ladder was soon imitated by other manufacturer.

Throughout the years, the Seagrave Corporation has come up with a steady stream of new ideas. In 1912, in the days of rotary or piston pumps, Seagrave's invention of a centrifugal pump capable of discharging 600 to 1,000 g.pm. and equipped with an automatic pressure gauge was hailed as a great success.

The same year as Pirsch and American, he manufactured a hydraulically operated ladder.

Seagrave's concern for the safety of firemen on board their fire engines led him, in 1935, to adopt the closed cab. Close on the trail of American LaFrance, he was the second manufacturer to offer a full range of chassis equipped with the cabover.

Although ladders remained his main interest throughout his life, the corporation which bears his name has also produced elevating platforms with special features.

One in particular is 90 ft, long and articulated in two places rather than one, like most of its current competitors.

Seagrave makes every possible type of fire engine; pumpers of all categories, aerial ladders, elevating platforms and rescue squad trucks.

Rescue squad trucks are widely used by American fire departments, and are highly effective in

Bottom: Pirsch is famous for its ladders, and was among the first to manufacture the 100-footer.

Top: A rescue squad truck equipped by Gertenslager.

all types of rescue operations. They combine the functions of compressors, power ventilating units (for the dispersion of toxic fumes), and can also carry several firemen. Because they can hold enormous amounts of equipment, their popularity is on the increase. All are custom-built, according to the special needs of any given fire department. Although they are usually mounted on standard commercial chassis, special chassis can be used also. For this reason, Seagrave sells a great number of these rescue squad trucks to various distributors, particularly to Gerstenlager, the largest supplier of "squads" in the world.

Swab, Pierce, Emergency One, Saulsbury, Bruco, Indiana and Hamerley are other manufacturers of rescue vehicles of this type.

Rescue squad trucks are used not only by fire departments but by other emergency services, for instance those operated by insurance companies, which are sent to protect property in case of fire, and investigate such devices as sprinklers, fire extinguishers and fireproof doors.

In 1963, Seagrave was taken over by the FWD Corporation, a longtime manufacturer of all-purpose heavyweight ground vehicles; since 1965, all operations have been based in Clintonville, Wisconsin.

Sutphen, often considered a newcomer in the field, has in fact been active in the fire-fighting industry since 1890. The relative obscurity of this company, which is based in Seagrave's former territory in Columbus, Ohio, is due to the fact that for many years it produced only the most traditional fire engines, without any special or innovative features. In 1963, however, Sutphen became known for the Aerial Tower.

This aluminum telescopic boom, made of four latticed components, has a bucket payload capacity of

over 1,100 lbs and is fed by two high-pressure monitor nozzles. Compared to the traditional 100 ft, ladder platform which can carry no more than 375 lbs (and is fed by only one monitor nozzle), the Aerial Tower by Sutphen supports unbelievably heavy weights. For this reason it has become extremely successful and is serious competition for Mack's Aerialscope. The first models of this type were 65 ft high; they were later made in 85 and 90 ft lengths before reaching the full 100 ft.

The standard model is mounted on a triple-axle chassis with a cabover and diesel engine; in most cases, it is also equipped with a 1 000 g.p.m. pump. If desired, the Aerial Tower can be mounted on massproduced chassis.

Although the Sutphen Fire Equipment Company is best known for the Aerial Tower, it also manufactures pumpers.

Grumman Emergency Products has qualified as a veteran since its merger with Howe-Oren, a company long known for its quality fire-fighting apparatus.

In 1961, Howe Fire Apparatus took over Oren Roanoke, then Coast Apparatus in 1965. The merger with Grumman in 1976 was made in an attempt to diversify that company's activities.

Of these manufacturers, Howe Fire Apparatus has the longest history, having entered the field as early as 1872. B.J.C. Howe's first creation was a horse-drawn pump with an unusual system that soon became very popular. When the horses arrived on the scene of the fire, they were unharnessed, placed in a circle, then reharnessed to the pump. By trotting around the pump in circles, they could activate the piston. The same work could be accomplished by no less than twenty men!

This uniquely American procedure was greatly developed, but was never adopted in other countries.

Howe was among the first to develop and automotive pump, in 1908. For many years he equipped Model T Fords, Reos, Dodges, Lincolns and Diamonds. In 1930, he finally manufactured his own chassis, the Defender.

In 1971, in collaboration with the International Harvester Company (the largest truck manufacturer in the United States), Howe developed a new cabover chassis for fire engines. They also designed a special cab for this chassis for the particular needs of fire departments.

During its long career, Howe-Oren won the staunch support of a great many small fire departments; this loyalty contributed greatly to the company's success.

Grumman Emergency Products is a division of Grumman Allied Indus-

tries, known throughout the world for its carrier based aircraft and its lunar modules. Sensing that the aerospatial industry was bound to slow down in future years, Grumman decided to enter the field of fire-fighting vehicles.

The apparatus born of the union with Howe-Oren have been baptized Tigercat, Firecat, Aerialcat and so forth, following Grumman's traditional practice of giving feline names to its US Navy fighter planes. If it's a "cat", it's always a Grumman.

With Howe-Oren's long experience in the fire-fighting field and Grumman's advanced technology, the combined talents of these companies can answer all the needs of every possible kind of fire department, from airport crash units to the smallest volunteer force in the smallest town.

On this 100-ft. European-style ladder truck, the turntable is placed at the rear and the ladder is built to rest on top of the cab.

PIERCE, OSHKOSH

A 1,250 g.p.m. Pierce pump is mounted on a White chassis. White, mainly associated with Volvo, supplies very few fire departments in the United States.

Wide-diameter hoses are increasingly being used as pumps grow more powerful. This 1,750 g.p.m. Hendrickson-Pierce carries three types: flat hoses can be seen behind the cab, a booster hose-reel in the middle, and two more flat hoses on enormous motorized hose-reels at the back.

Water tankers are rarely used in the United States, and look very much like pumpers. This Ford Louiseville, equipped by Pierce, holds 1,250 gal. of water.

A Squrt is mounted on an elegant Oshkosh-Pirsch.

In 1917, when Pierce began operations, it concentrated mostly on body-work for commercial vehicles. Two decades later, this company took a new direction and, for many years, manufactured equipment for fire engines made by other firms.

In 1968, the Pierce Manufacturing Co began to equip its own vehicles and created the Suburban series. The most popular model was mounted on a Ford C, and equipped with a 1 000 g.p.m. Waterous pump and a 750 gal. water tank. True to its name, the Suburban was designed for use in large American suburbs. This pumper could also be mounted on other chassis (such as International and GMC), and equipped with larger pumps and tanks.

Pierce's 4 x 4 and 4 x 2 mini-pumpers, mounted on Dodge or International pickup trucks, have become extremely popular. They are increasingly being used for fires in parking lots, shopping malls or on highways, and can also combat brush fires. On certain models, pumps can discharge 250 g.p.m. while the vehicle is stationary or in motion, and water tanks hold 250 gal.; other extinguishing agents, such as dry powder of foam, can be provided.

Attack pumpers of a more powerful type are called Minutemen; the origin of this name takes us back two centuries.

At the time of the American Revolution, militia were formed by groups of volunteers who, when not called upon to fight the British, would resume their normal everyday activities. When the enemy was near, a series of light signals were relayed from house to house.

The men who perfected this simple and efficient system were baptized "minutemen" because of the remarkable speed with which these otherwise placid farmers and trad-

*T*hese two manufacturing companies, based in Appleton and Oshkosh, Wisconsin, are only a few miles apart. Because of their close proximity to each other, they have occasionally found it convenient to work together, but there is another reason. In 1981, Pierce equipped the one hundredth Oshkosh chassis, a relatively large number considering that these were all heavy-duty vehicles, and that Pierce had only entered the fire-fighting industry in 1968. Oshkosh has become famous for these giant vehicles, whereas Pierce is best-known for its mini-pumpers.

esmen could mobilize into a good-sized fighting force.

Many of these fire engines carry the emblem of the minuteman, complete with lantern and large hat. For most Americans, the word has come to symbolize readiness to perform a civic duty.

All heavy vehicles equipped by Pierce (pumpers, tankers, rescue trucks, aerial ladders, elevating platforms and Squrts) are mounted on chassis by International, Ford, Dodge, Duplex GMC, FWD, Hendrickson and Oshkosh. Since 1979, however, Pierce has been manufacturing its own chassis, the Pierce Arrow.

For lovers of old automobiles, the name Pierce Arrow brings to mind the luxurious cars that were built in Buffalo until 1938. The Pierce Manufacturing Co had bought the rights to use this brand-name for its chassis.

Pierce Arrow pumpers are equipped with 1,000 to 2,000 g.p.m. pumps and have a tank capacity of 500 to 750 gal.

The basic Oshkosh chassis is mounted with aerial ladders and elevating platforms.

The largest order ever received by Pierce or any other manufacturer came from Saudi-Arabia in 1974: a total of eight hundred and eighty-six fire vehicles, all mounted on GMC chassis, were bought for $ 54 million. These included pumpers, mini-pumpers, water tankers, special apparatus for chemical fires equipped with water, foam and dry powder guns, ladder and platform trucks, mobile cranes, rescue trucks, radioactive detector units, ambulances, laboratories and surgical units mounted on semi-trailers, repair vans, generator carriers and canteen and kitchen wagons.

This transaction, aimed at replacing

The Pierce Arrow brand name recalls the luxurious automobiles of the Twenties and Thirties.

Saudi-Arabia's outdated English fleet, was the largest ever recorded in peacetime.

Pierce was not in any position to fill this order on its own and, for the sake of its own future, had to honor other commitments. And so it was decided that a special industrial group would be formed especially for the occasion. This group, called the Engineering Equipment Company, included Pierce, American LaFrance, Snorker, Fire-Tec and, lastly, the Calumet Coach Company, which specializes in canteen wagons and laboratories.

Of the eight hundred and eighty-six vehicles, all of which were painted yellow, a number were sold by Saudi Arabia to neighboring countries.

Oshkosh, founded the same year as Pierce, borrowed its name from the town in which the company is based, a few miles south of Appleton.

The Chief of the Menominee tribe after whom this town was christened, would have been surprised to see the giant apparatus manufactured by Oshkosh, all sporting his name. The Oshkosh Truck Corporation, created by B.A. Mostling and William Besserdick, formerly of FWD, manufactures special heavy-duty vehicles designed to travel long distances on rough ground; they are used for oil detection and to transport nuclear wastes. Oshkosh also makes tank-carriers, snowplows and transit mixers.

Although the manufacturing of fire engines is only a secondary line for this company, Oshkosh was producing them as early as 1920.

These vehicles, noted for their size, originality and power, are mostly used in commercial and military airports.

Oshkosh fire engines are built to transport enormous quantities of water and other extinguishing

THE PORT OF NEW YORK AUTHORITY

agents; they must have high acceleration characteristics and be able to travel on the frequently rough grounds of the areas surrounding airports.

These requirements are satisfied by the many different types of vehicles built by this company. The M-23 weighs fifty nine tons, carries a pump rated at 3,000 g.p.m., 6,000 gal. of water and 500 gal. of emulsifiers. It can reach its maximum speed of 50 m.p.h. in fifty seconds. The M-15 (4,000 gal. capacity) and the M-12 (3,250 gal.) have even more rapid acceleration.

Although its best client is the US Air Force, Oshkosh sells special fire engines to most large American airports: Memphis, Tucson, Los Angeles, San Francisco, etc.

The lighter-weight T model, also noted for its excellent performance, is less expensive than the M model and is growing increasingly popular.

Besides these special vehicles, Oshkosh also manufactures more traditional A models, which can be equipped with pumps, aerial ladders, elevating platforms, aerial towers or Squrts. They are supplied to Pierce, Van Pelt, Pirsch, Snorkel, Fire Apparatus and Ladder Towers.

The L model has a low silhouette chassis and can measure less than six feet from the ground to the top of the cab.

Most of these vehicles are made in Wisconsin, but Oshkosh now has factories in South Africa and Australia.

An 85-ft. telescopic platform by Ladder Towers is mounted on a low-silhouette Oshkosh.

CROWN, FMC-VAN PELT

A High-Ranger platform equipped by Van Pelt is mounted on an International chassis; the town, of course, is in California.

The Crown Firecoach Corporation, originally known only on the West Coast, has in recent years sold many vehicles in other parts of the United States. Most of its pumps are rated at 1,500 g.p.m.

Calavar's Firebird
attacks a major
Sacramento fire.
125-ft. models can
carry a 1,000 l.b.
payload.

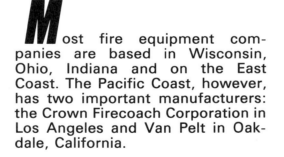

Most fire equipment companies are based in Wisconsin, Ohio, Indiana and on the East Coast. The Pacific Coast, however, has two important manufacturers: the Crown Firecoach Corporation in Los Angeles and Van Pelt in Oakdale, California.

Although Crown apparatus is mostly used on the West Coast and in Hawaii, this brand is slowly growing popular in other States.

The volunteer fire department of Montvale, New Jersey, was the first to break tradition by purchasing three Crown fire engines; until then, no apparatus by this manufacturer had been seen east of the Missisippi.

The Crown Firecoach Corporation, noted for the fine quality of its fire apparatus, has traditionally supplied the city and country of Los Angeles. It was created in 1949 as a subsidiary of the Crown Coach Corporation, which specializes in public transportation vehicles,

school buses, utility trucks and motor homes. Fire engines are equipped with cabs greatly similar to those of these other vehicles, and are made in relatively small quantities — two or three dozen each year.

Crown Firecoach manufactures one standard model, which can be mounted with every possible kind of apparatus; each vehicle is made

FIRE STATION NO. 80

FIRE
783

80

to order, and delivery time is never less than fifteen months.

Elevating platforms, Squrts and Tele-Squrts can be mounted on these vehicles. From 1966 to 1980, Crown bought aerial ladders from Maxim, but has since abandoned this type of apparatus.

As can be expected, Crown Firecoach has filled many special orders

for the Los Angeles Fire Department. In 1963, the city decided to replace its American LaFrance Metropolitan Duplex pumpers, which had been in service since 1938, and bought a new fleet from Crown. These enormous new pumpers were rated at 2,000 g.p.m., which at the time was considerable.

This kind of apparatus has become

In America, many city fire departments are also expected to combat airport fires. The Yankee, seen here protecting the Los Angeles Airport, was built in this city.

59

Like most forest services in the U.S.A., the Los Angeles Fire Department uses bulldozers to combat forest fires. The truck pictured above is an elongated version of the standard Crown pumper.

An F.M.C. pumper on an International chassis. F.M.C., as can clearly be seen by the lettering on the cab door, specializes in high-pressure pumps.

Preceding pages: Like many other fire equipment companies, F.M.C. manufactures its own chassis, but is best known for its high-pressure pumps. Some F.M.C.-Bean pumps are rated as high as 870 p.s.i.!

standard, however, which gives us an idea of the race being waged among American fire companies for bigger and more powerful pumps.

In 1981, the fire equipment industry was taken by surprise by the decision of the Oakdale Fire Department to order a large number of fire engines from the Van Pelt Company; for the last ten years, this California city had been equipped exclusively by Crown, Seagrave and American LaFrance.

Ten pumpers mounted on Spartan Motors chassis and rated at 1,750 g.p.m. were to be delivered by F.M.C.-Van Pelt.

This company, known on the Pacific Coast since 1925, has in recent years been the largest supplier of fire equipment in that part of the United States. Most of its chassis are made by Ford, GMC, Duplex and Oshkosh; for a time, the Oakdale company manufac-

tured its own chassis, but soon abandoned the practice.

Van Pelt uses telescopic platforms made by Ladder Towers, Inc., and High-Ranger articulated aerial towers.

Pumps are provided by Hale and, in most cases, by F.M.C. This is hardly surprising considering the fact that Van Pelt was taken over in 1978 by the fire equipment division of the Food Machinery Company of Tipton, Indiana; this negotiation was made by F.M.C. in an attempt to sell its apparatus on the West Coast.

Under the trade name John Bean, F.M.C. has been a pioneer in the manufacturing of high-pressure pumps in the United States. It now offers a wide range of fire engines mounted on different brands of chassis as well as its own. Among these are large capacity tanker trucks (255 gal.), "econopac" pumpers rated at 750 to 1,000 g.p.m.

with 750 gal. tank capacity, and "quick attack" pumpers, equipped with high-pressure pumps.

Attack pumpers, as their name indicates, are the first to arrive on the scene and attack the fire while the larger pumpers are being prepared for operations. This kind of maneuver is being used more and more in the United States.

F.M.C. is universally known for its farm machinery and is the largest manufacturer of tracked army vehicles in the world.

Another important Pacific Coast fire equipment manufacturer, taken over in 1965 by Howe-Oren, was the Coast Apparatus Company of Martinez, California.

Finally, we cannot fail to mention the Calavar Corporation, of Sante Fe Springs: its 150 ft. Firebird, with a bucket payload capacity of 750 lbs, is the highest aerial tower in the world.

This quick survey of American fire engines can do little more than suggest the infinite variety of fire apparatus to be found on this continent. Reasons for this are the enormous size of the United States and the great numbers of small manufacturers.

Fabulous as they may be, these fire engines are also very expensive. The price of a standard pumper is in the range of $ 75,000 to $ 80,000; a ladder truck can cost up to $ 200,000.

This explains the low replacement rate of fire engines in America.

This typical West Coast pumper was made by Crown for the Los Angeles Fire Department.

BIBLIOGRAPHY

American Fire Engines since 1900, by Walter P. McCall; Crestline Publishing.
Fire Engines Firefighters, by Paul C. Ditzel; Crown Publishers.
The Complete Book of Fire Engines; Louis Weber, publisher.
American Trucks of the Seventies, by Elliott Kahn; Warne, publisher.
Collecting and Restoring Antique Fire Engines, by Robert Lichty; Tab Books, Inc.
Fire Company Apparatus and Procedures, by Lawrence W. Erven; Glencoe Press.

ACKNOWLEDGEMENTS

We wish to express our thanks to the following companies: American LaFrance, Emergency One, Mack, Pirsch, Pierce, Boardman, Darley, Maxim, Oshkosh, Ladder Towers, Grumman; and to Messieurs Boileau, Bengston, Havard, Horb and Martineau.
The author would gratefully like to acknowledge the contribution of Mr. J.A. Toomey, one of the best and most talented American photographers of fire engines, and his invaluable help in the preparation of this work.

PHOTOGRAPHIC CREDITS

J.A. Toomey, pages 3, 5, 9, 15, 16, 17, 19, 21, 25, 28, 29, 35, 39, 40, 41, 45, 48, 49, 51, 55, 61.
Bengston, pages 42, 62.
New York Fire Department, pages 6, 30, 31, 47.
Havard Collection, pages 16, 43, 56.
Mack, pages 24, 25.
Emery, page 25.
Oshkosh, page 53.
Calavar, page 57.
Martineau, page 56.
Los Angeles Fire Department, pages 59, 62, 63.
Emergency One, pages 33, 36, 37.
Dubois, page 49.
American LaFrance, pages 13, 17, 18, 22, cover photograph.
Grumman, page 40.
Maxim, page 23.
Darley, pages 7, 11.
All rights reserved, pages 43, 54.
Cover photograph: An American LaFrance Century pumper, with a deck gun mounted on top.

This 1984 edition published by Crescent Books, distributed by Crown Publishers, Inc.

Originally published in French under the title
Les Fabuleux Véhicules d'Incendie Américains.

Printed in France and bound in France.

Library of Congress Cataloging in Publication Data.

Mallet, Janette
Great American Fire Engines
Translation of : Les Fabuleux Véhicules d'Incendie Américains.
1. Fire Engines—United States— History. I. Title.
TH9371.M33613 1984   628.9'25   84-7735
ISBN 0-517-448289

h g f e d c b a

Achevé d'imprimer sur les presses
de Berger-Levrault à Nancy
779448 — Dépôt légal juillet 1984
Imprimé en France